Inside Out and All About

Laura McGinnis

BookLeaf
Publishing

India | USA | UK

Presentation by *BookLeaf Publishing*

Web: www.bookleafpub.com

E-mail: info@bookleafpub.com

ISBN: 9789363317246

First edition 2024

To Tom, Mike, and Marg

who keep things interesting.

*I wouldn't change a thing (except maybe a
poem or two).*

ACKNOWLEDGEMENT

Thanks to Dean, Jeanmarie, Marcy, and the Cleveland Museum of Art.

Missing Muse

Words flooded so easily,
        too easily,
from mind
to fingers
pouring by a favorite pen
across the black lines
that ribbed a fresh white page.

What to do
when the words stop
when the muse is gone
when the hand, fingers, pen,
want to write
but the lake is dry,
nothing flows from the source?

When voice and heart are silent?

Butterfly Effect

Dear Someone who I hope is out there
but whom I hope never to meet,

I hope you're doing something grand
       just because I flapped my little butterfly
wings.

I hope that I have somehow made your world
       a better, safer, lovelier, more serene
place

because of something small I once did:
       a smile, a good word, some thoughtless
deed

that resonated with the universe,
       if only for one brief moment

to settle some dust, water a flower,
       wipe a tear, induce a giggle.

I wish you nothing but all the best,
       but if we were to meet,

If I knew the impact of my small act,

came face-to-face with the results

I fear it would take away the magic,
         the wonder, the miracle.

And so I am happy not knowing
         yet believing

that you are out there somewhere
         having a good life

and never knowing why.

With all my love and best wishes,

         Me.

Sedoka

Do you know I tried
with perfect imperfection
to do the right things?

Do you know you did
with imperfect perfection
the best that you could?

Abcedarian Bees Circling Dandelions

A rose
By any other name
Could smell as sweet but
Don't dismiss the humble dandelion.
Every spring my yard Is
Filled with a
Golden carpet, buzzing with
Honeybees
Intent on their vital
Job: facilitating sex between consenting flowers.
Knowing how important this job is,
Let them have their fun.
Mow the lawn a few weeks later
Not when the yellow blooms are just
Open. Don't feel bad about
Putting off the first cut of the year.
Quite the opposite:
Reward yourself for being
Sensitive to the needs of
Those little creatures
Under your thoughtful care.
Very soon your patience
Will be rewarded with liquid gold
eXquisite sweet amber honey

Yours for the small price of Spring idleness:
Zero cost, yummy goodness.

Introspection?

What is inside you?
      What makes you tick?
            What is gnawing to get out?

Wanderlust?
The need to be somewhere new,
      somewhere else?

Passion?
      The drive to succeed,
         To have an impact?

Dreams, wishes unfulfilled,
      Asking when will it be my turn?

Hunger
      for justice,
      for mercy,
         for a good burrito?

Or is it that burrito
      and the margarita that came with it
gnawing to get out?

Introspection?
    or indigestion?

Accountancy of Benevolence

One good deed deserves another.
An eye for an eye.
Turn the other cheek.
I owe you one.

Do my assets match my liabilities?
Have I given as good as I got?

Why must life be transactional?

Plant some seeds.
Sprinkle some gold dust.
Hold a door.
Practice random acts of kindness.
Raise the level of good in the world.

Global warming of hearts and souls
would not be a bad thing.

(for Dean)

Protest Poem - Almost

There's a protest poem in me,
too skittish to come out,
too big to ignore,
too frightening
to make words.
It scares
me.

Happy Thoughts

Rainbows
Butterflies
Lightningbugs
A goldfinch in my wildflowers
A nest of baby robins on my porch
Happy thoughts
Think happy thoughts

A good pen
Bunny butts
Fingerpainting
Warm fudge brownies with french vanilla ice
cream
A rippling creek stippled by sunlight that glints
through lacy leaves
Happy thoughts
Think happy thoughts

Petrichor (look it up)
A new book by a favorite author
A birthday divisible by 5, 10, 25, 100
Fresh sheets on a hot summer night after a cool
shower

The lingering aroma of my grandmother's Jean
Nate' on handkerchiefs discovered in an
unmarked box of hand-me-downs
Happy thoughts
Think happy thoughts

Marcy

13

Motherhood is a wondrous whirlwind
As days run long and years run short.
Rock your love created by love,
Capture memories while you can.
Yesterdays turn to tomorrows too fast.

Global Warming Feast

I strewed wildflower seeds along the back fence
for the pollinators, like the good global citizen I
strive to be.
The deer thought the salad was delicious,

but, small victory:
a goldfinch has arrived,
a flitting yellow belly
among the stunted weeds.

Big Butler Fair

Shots rang out.
Look about.
Another came
Six more the same

Stage rushed.
Candidate hushed
Bloodied ear
Looks of fear

"What now?"
supporters howl.
Conspiracies fly.
Who knows why?

Dakota Woods 1

Cabin in the woods,
doe and fawn able along:
mountain traffic jam.

Dakota Woods 2

17

Morning mists settle,
sunlight glints stippled shadows.
Green, green everywhere!

Dakota Woods 3

My place to be me
destination and retreat
cabin in the woods

Haikai

He laughs at my jokes
even those corny and bad
this one's a keeper

(untitled)

In Hiroshima
    I shoveled snow in August
neighbors ashes drift

Tanka

Another year passes.
The journey of forever
    started with a kiss
    and a promise so immense
who could fathom it?

Two-thirds of our lives,
    looking back, just a moment.
Unpack memories,
    priceless gems and worthless stones
but still room for more.

– June 22, 2024

The Cleveland Thinker 1

I am the watcher,
   I am The Thinker,
looking out,
   gazing in,
consumed by the chaos around me
   consumed by the chaos within me,
oblivious to the chaos within me
   oblivious to the chaos around me
searching for meaning,
   searching for meaning.

Still Searching

I'll start with just a line or two
        then see what else my pen can do.
A third line might a tercet make
        but look, a quatrain overtakes.

Writing in forms can be such fun
        but now the poetry challenge's done.

The last day calls for freeform verse.
        I doubt my poems could get much
worse.

And still it is my muse I seek.
She's trapped inside
        this meter,
        these rhymes,
        syllable counts (that don't really count):
scaffolding that holds the words in place.

Scaffolding holds the world in place.
But what magic holds the scaffold?

The Cleveland Thinker 2

What thought so deep?
What image so compelling?
You haven't noticed
    your feet have been blown off?

What fills your head,
your immutable, inscrutable head,
that your personal crisis
    matters not a whit in your world?

Disfigured, yes,
but life goes on.
The sun still rises and sets,
    burning and chilling your bronze.

There are more important matter
than an ankle over here, toes over there.
Intact from the knees up,
    cogitation continues uninterrupted.

This puny avatar
stares up at you
wondering what moment of thought
    did Rodin capture?

www.ingramcontent.com/pod-product-compliance
Lightning Source LLC
LaVergne TN
LVHW021349200726
843509LV00014B/2752